Whispers Across the Wilds:

Poems from the Breath of the Elements

Brandon Michaels

Whispers Across the Wilds:

Poems from the Breath of the Elements

All Rights Reserved

Copyright © 2026 by Brandon Michaels

All Rights Reserved

Copyright ©2026

Nudous Publishing, LLC

www.nudouspublishing.com
info@nudouspublishing.com

Digital ISBN: 978-1-970523-09-6

Paperback ISBN: 978-1-970523-10-2

Author Guilds Reg #: 291429

This is a work of fiction. Names, characters, businesses, places, events, locales, and incidents are either the products of the author's imagination or used in a fictitious manner. Any resemblance to actual persons, living or dead, or actual events is purely coincidental.

This book is protected under the copyright laws of the United States of America. Any reproduction or other unauthorized use of the material or artwork herein is prohibited without the author's or publisher's express written permission.

Table of Contents

Introduction: Let the Wild Whisper

Before the root, before the wave, the wind,
The earth was speaking softly from within.

In stone and ash, in river, frost, and flame,
It called each living thing by secret name.

The forests breathe in shadows, bark, and light,
The deserts guard what vanished from our sight.

The oceans keep the tears of time and tide,
While mountains lift the soul where heavens hide.

The grasslands open thought beyond the far,
The wetlands mirror who we truly are.

The ice preserves what memory cannot hold,
The fire below makes broken spirits bold.

So enter now where every silence speaks,
And hear the truths the restless wild still seeks.

Forest

The Language of Bark and Shadow

Beneath the bark the old roots softly croon,
They murmur secrets to the silver moon.

In woven dark where patient shadows glade,
The elder pines repeat what time has made.

Through buried veins their silent warnings flow,
From root to root where only stillness knows.

Each cedar bends beneath the starlit sky,
To share the truths that never fully die.

The oaks remember storms of wind and fire,
And pass them down like breath from choir to choir.

No tree beneath the canopy's alone,
Its pulse still beats through earth and living stone.

So bark and shadow speak in hidden time,
The forest turns their breath to sacred rhyme.

Where the Ferns Remember

Where fallen leaves sink deep in earthen bed,
The ferns unfold where older seasons bled.

They cradle names the forest will not keep,
Yet hold them still in roots that wander deep.

Each frond uncurls like fingers made of grace,
And brushes time across the darkened place.

The rain returns to wake what once lay still,
Old whispers rising soft beneath the hill.

In every rot there stirs a hidden birth,
A green remembrance breathing through the earth.

The past lies warm beneath the moss and rain,
Then blooms again through sorrow, loss, and pain.

So every step upon the forest floor,
Awakes the ghosts of all who came before.

Canopy Cathedral

The redwoods rise like pillars carved from stone,
Their towering silence crowns the woods alone.

Through emerald glass the golden sunbeams pour,
Like holy fire spilled across the floor.

Each branch becomes an arch of living grace,
A vaulted hymn suspended over space.

The hush beneath them stills the restless mind,
As if the wind itself has turned benign.

The moss below becomes a velvet pew,
Where earth and spirit meet in shaded dew.

No priest is here, no hand has shaped this spire,
Yet every leaf still lifts the soul up higher.

I stand beneath their blessing, small yet whole,
While filtered light pours mercy through my soul.

Lichen's Slow Gospel

On weathered bark and stone it learns to stay,
A patient hymn that time cannot dismay.

It asks no sunlit field, no fertile ground,
Yet builds its quiet kingdom all around.

In muted green it writes its tender creed,
That life grows slow wherever hearts still heed.

Each fragile bloom upon the granite's face,
Becomes a testament to stubborn grace.

The storms may lash, the bitter winters press,
Still lichen answers hardship with its yes.

It clings through years no mortal hand can trace,
And turns bare ruin into sacred space.

So let me learn from what the ages show,
That strength need never hurry still to grow.

A Root for Every Memory

Beneath the oak where childhood laughter stayed,
The roots still hold the paths our footsteps made.

Each buried thread of sorrow, joy, and name,
Runs through the soil yet never fades the same.

A father's voice still lingers in the pine,
A mother's warmth still lives in cedar's line.

The years may strip the branches bare with snow,
Yet deeper still the oldest memories grow.

Each place we loved sends tendrils through the ground,
In every ring the ghosts of home are found.

The forest keeps what time cannot destroy,
Our grief, our love, our innocence, our joy.

So every root that twists beneath my feet,
Returns the ones I lost in whispers sweet.

Mosslight

A green hush gathers where the shadows sleep,
And spills its glow through hollows dark and deep.

The forest floor breathes softly under light,
A muted flame that turns the dimness bright.

Each stone is dressed in velvet, cool and slow,
As if the earth itself has learned to glow.

The fallen limbs wear emerald like a crown,
Where silent grace keeps every sorrow down.

No sound is lost, it settles in the green,
Half lived in memory, half in waking dream.

Here life still stirs beneath the quiet air,
In whispered roots and spores that linger there.

So let me rest where all things fade to light,
And breathe the moss that turns the dark to bright.

Desert

Bones Beneath the Dunes

Beneath the dunes lie remnants lost to time,
Their fractured shapes made sacred by the climb.

The wind moves slow across the buried dead,
And smooths the names from every silent bed.

Old bones once carried breath through flesh and fire,
Now rest below the sun's unyielding pyre.

The sand remakes what sorrow could not keep,
And folds the broken further into sleep.

Each grain becomes a keeper of the past,
Reshaping grief through tempests fierce and fast.

What once was feared is weathered into grace,
A vanished life erased without a trace.

Yet still beneath the dunes their stories stay,
Waiting for wind to speak them back one day.

The Sun that Forgot to Set

The horizon burned beneath a molten sky,
Where hours withered slow and would not die.

The sun stood still above the blistered plain,
A watchful eye that offered only pain.

The dunes stretched on like waves of sleeping fire,
Each step consumed by heat and fierce desire.

No dusk arrived to cool the trembling air,
Only a brightness sharp enough to sear.

The shadows shrank to nothing at my feet,
Erased beneath the endless pulse of heat.

Time lost its shape in amber, glare, and haze,
A world suspended in unending blaze.

At last I learned the desert's ruthless truth,
Some suns outlive the limits born of youth.

Scars of Wind and Stone

The canyon walls bear marks the ages wrote,
Each jagged line a weathered, wordless note.

The wind has carved its sorrow into face,
Yet left behind a fierce and solemn grace.

The cliffs stand split where old eruptions tore,
Still holding fast against the desert's roar.

Each ridge recalls the fury of the past,
Yet rises stronger for what could not last.

The stone wears pain like armor in the sun,
Proof every wound can harden and still run.

What time has cut, the silence makes it whole,
A scarred horizon stitched across the soul.

So wind and stone together teach this land,
That broken things can still endure and stand.

Mirage Gospel

A silver lake appeared beyond the sand,
A shining promise just beyond my hand.

I chased its light through waves of bending air,
But found no mercy waiting for me there.

The desert knows the shape of thirst and need,
And feeds the eye with visions born of greed.

Each trembling gleam became a whispered prayer,
A holy lie dissolved in open air.

What looked like refuge vanished into heat,
A phantom hymn retreating with my feet.

Still something in the emptiness rang true,
The longing was the sermon I walked through.

For some pursuits are holy in their loss,
A mirage gospel written by the cross.

Nothing Grows Here But Fire

The cracked earth split beneath a ruthless flame,
No tender root could rise and stay the same.

The wind blew hot with embers sharp as grief,
And burned away the comfort of belief.

No bloom survived the hunger of this place,
Only the ash of what once sought out grace.

Yet in the blaze there lived a fiercer seed,
A will to endure beyond all want and need.

The desert taught that softness cannot last,
When every mercy's swallowed by the blast.

Still something stronger kindled in the pyre,
A harder heart fed only into fire.

So from the ruin scorched beneath the sun,
I learned some lives are forged, not gently won.

The Silence that Swallowed Sound

No echo lived beneath the open sky,
Each word I spoke dissolved before reply.

The dunes stretched wide in mute and endless sleep,
A stillness vast enough to bury deep.

The wind moved on without a voice or name,
And left the world untouched, unchanged, the same.

No bird, no stream, no branch remained to stir,
Only the hush of heat and endless blur.

In that great void my heartbeat grew more clear,
The only sound that proved that I was here.

The desert took the noise I used to hide,
And left me standing with my stripped-down mind.

At last I heard the truth beneath the sun,
When all sound dies, the self becomes the one.

Tundra & Ice

The Shape of Frozen Wind

The wind cut clean across the open white,
And carved the air to edges hard and bright.

Each breath emerged in crystals thin and slow,
Then vanished in the waiting drifts below.

The frost gave form to what the eye can't keep,
Sharp ridges built where silent currents sleep.

The cold itself became a sculptor's hand,
And shaped the emptiness across the land.

No mercy moved within that brittle sky,
Only the frozen breath of winter's eye.

Yet in its harshness there was something clear,
A truth that only stillness makes appear.

So wind and ice together drew their line,
And taught the air itself could be design.

Footprints in Permafrost

A line of steps lay pressed beneath the snow,
Still marked where someone vanished long ago.

The frozen earth refused to let them fade,
But kept their weight in silence where they stayed.

Each print became a map of breath and bone,
A proof that once this white had not been lone.

The years moved on, yet cold denied release,
Preserving motion in unbroken peace.

No voice remained to tell me who passed by,
Only the shape of absence in the ice.

The tundra keeps what warmer lands would lose,
A memory the frost itself still chooses.

So every step half-buried in the frost,
Reminds the earth no journey's ever lost.

Long Light, Long Shadow

The daylight lingered far beyond its time,
A pale unending stretch of silver shine.

No dusk arrived to grant the spirit rest,
The sky stayed fixed like weight upon my chest.

Then months would turn and darkness took its place,
A longer shadow draped across the waste.

The nights grew vast, yet somehow softly kind,
A shelter for the fractures of the mind.

In endless light I learned what longing meant,
In endless dark I learned what stillness lent.

The seasons here do not so much depart,
They settle slow like weather in the heart.

So long light, long shadow, both remain as one,
The soul survives by waiting for the sun.

A Prayer in the White

The snow stretched wide like untouched sacred page,
A silent hymn preserved from age to age.

No road remained, no mark to guide my feet,
Only the holy hush of endless sheet.

The white held room for every thought unsaid,
Each longing drifting softly through my head.

No walls confined the prayer I could not name,
The open cold received it just the same.

The stillness answered not with voice but peace,
A quiet vast enough to grant release.

In all that blank I felt my spirit clear,
As if the frost had stripped away all fear.

So in the white where solitude takes form,
I found a silence deeper than a storm.

The Ice Remembers

Beneath the blue the oldest moments stay,
Locked in the frost where time has lost its way.

A touch, a name, a love once warm with breath,
Now sleeps in crystal, untouched even by death.

The glacier keeps what sorrow could not bury,
Its frozen chambers hold what hearts still carry.

Each layer pressed beneath the weight of years,
Preserves the salt of ancient joys and tears.

No fire can reach what winter has confessed,
The cold becomes a keeper of the blessed.

Even grief, once sharp enough to break,
Grows still and clear beneath the silver lake.

So ice remembers what the flesh must leave,
And guards the truths we ache to still believe.

Glacier Song

The mountain hummed beneath its frozen weight,
A song so slow it seemed to challenge fate.

The glacier moved in silence, deep and wide,
A buried hymn no mortal ear could hide.

Its voice was not of words but stone and strain,
A grinding psalm beneath the fields of plain.

Each inch it crossed rewrote the sleeping land,
With patient force no life could countermand.

The ages passed within its crystal throat,
Yet still it carried every buried note.

No rush, no fear, no need to prove its might,
It shaped the world by moving out of sight.

So in that song too deep for sound to keep,
I heard the ancient earth still dream in sleep.

Grassland

The Horizon We Chased

We ran where golden fields met endless sky,
Still sure the distant line was drawing nigh.

The tall grass bent beneath our laughing feet,
As if the earth itself urged us to meet.

Each mile ahead became another mile,
A promise shining just beyond our trial.

The wind moved fast with freedom in its breath,
And filled our lungs with dreams untouched by death.

Yet every crest revealed more open land,
Another stretch we could not quite command.

The horizon kept the shape of all we sought,
A moving edge no hand has ever caught.

Still I remember how the chase felt true,
The world made wide by all we thought we knew.

Dandelion Sermons

The yellow blooms rose bright through common ground,
Small suns of grace the hurried seldom found.

They stood where stronger flowers would not stay,
Yet turned their fragile faces toward the day.

The wind arrived and broke them into flight,
A thousand prayers released in threads of white.

Each seed went forth with no demand for claim,
Trusting the air to carry forth its name.

They taught that beauty does not need to last,
To leave its truth long after it has passed.

The fields grew full from what the breeze had sown,
A quiet gospel scattered and unknown.

So now I bless the things that drift and part,
For small truths travel farthest in the heart.

The Wind Has a Spine

The wind bent grass in long unbroken rows,
A living back that shifted where it blows.

It carried dust, old voices, seed, and bone,
And crossed the fields as if it walked alone.

Each gust drew borders none could truly see,
Yet moved the shape of land and history.

It pressed against the fences, thin and worn,
And sang through wire like something half reborn.

The prairie learned to lean but never break,
To bend with every force the skies could make.

So stories traveled farther than the road,
Riding the spine of every moving gale.

I felt it pass right through my chest and skin,
A restless strength that carried worlds within.

Golden Miles

The grasses rolled in waves of amber light,
Each mile aglow beneath the lowering bright.

The road ran thin between the earth and sky,
A quiet thread where all our thoughts passed by.

No mountain broke the sweep of open land,
Only the fields like hope on every hand.

The same soft gold returned with every bend,
A repetition gentle as a friend.

The beauty lay in how it did not change,
A steady grace spread wide and sweetly strange.

Each mile became another breath of peace,
A promise that the ache in us could cease.

So I kept walking where the wheat winds smiled,
And found my heart made calm by golden mile.

Beneath the Tall Grass

The prairie swayed in golden waves above,
Yet hid below the pulse of fear and love.

The stems stood high and brushed against my knee,
A curtain drawn on what I could not see.

Small lives moved soft where sunlight could not fall,
Eyes bright and still beneath the rustling wall.

Old bones lay lost where roots had claimed their name,
And buried stories fed the earth the same.

The grass concealed both shelter and unknown,
A world of breath that lived beneath its grown.

I felt the watching silence at my feet,
A hidden life that made the fields complete.

So every open mile held secret birth,
The unseen heartbeat of the breathing earth.

A Sky With No Ceiling

Above the plains the heavens opened wide,
No wall of stone, no roof, no place to hide.

The blue stretched on beyond what sight could claim,
A boundless height untouched by fear or name.

The wind moved free through thought, breath, bone,
And taught the soul it need not stay confined.

Each cloud became a doorway into more,
A silent threshold with no final shore.

The prairie below seemed small beneath that span,
Yet somehow made more room for what I am.

In endless air the spirit learned to rise,
Unfastened from the weight of narrower skies.

So here beneath a sky with no true end,
I found the part of me too wide to bend.

Ocean

Salt Memory

The tide returned with whispers from the deep,
Old names dissolved in waters meant to keep.

Each wave carried fragments worn by time,
A grief made smooth by salt and rhythm's chime.

The sea remembers every ship that fell,
Each shattered mast, each storm, each final swell.

It keeps the tears of lovers cast away,
And folds them gently in the pull of bay.

No sorrow truly vanishes from foam,
It drifts in currents far from where we roam.

The salt upon my lips tasted of years,
A mingled trace of journeys, love, and tears.

So standing where the restless waters breathe,
I felt the ocean's memory rise beneath.

Where the Light Fails

Below the waves the blue began to fade,
The sun withdrew and left a deeper shade.

Each stroke pulled me through colder, darker sea,
Toward truths the surface never lets us see.

The brightness thinned to threads of trembling gray,
Then vanished where the light could never stay.

In that great depth the silence gathered near,
A pressure shaped from everything we fear.

The dark held forms that moved beyond my sight,
Half born of ocean, half of inward night.

Yet still I sank where hidden currents flow,
For some truths live where only shadows grow.

At last I learned beneath the failing glow,
The deepest parts are where we come to know.

A Thousand Mouths Below

The currents hummed beneath the rolling tide,
A chorus born where unseen voices hide.

The coral clicked in chambers made of stone,
A patient speech in tongues not wholly known.

Far off, the whales released their mournful cry,
A sound that seemed to bend the water's sky.

Each wave broke open with a different tone,
As if the sea refused to sing alone.

The kelp fields swayed like choirs in the deep,
Their rustling prayers what darker waters keep.

No single mouth could hold what oceans say,
It takes a thousand depths to shape one wave.

So standing still beside the breathing shore,
I heard the sea speak through forevermore.

Tide and Time

The tide moved in with patient, measured grace,
Then pulled away and left a changed-up place.

Each shell, each branch, each footprint by the shore,
Was claimed by waves and given back once more.

The sea keeps time in rhythms old and slow,
A clock of moonlit rise and undertow.

What love once leaves, the currents may return,
Though weathered by the years through which they turn.

No loss remains untouched by ebb and flow,
The deepest grief still learns the tides must go.

And what is gone may circle back one day,
In altered form, yet true in its own way.

So standing where the surf rewrites the sand,
I felt time move like water through my hand.

Speak, Whale-Born Silence

A whale's low call moved through the midnight sea,
A lonely hymn too vast for shore to see.

The sound rolled out through miles of moonless blue,
Then vanished where no answering voices grew.

The ocean held the beauty of that loss,
A silence deep enough to bear its cross.

No echo rose from caverns dark and wide,
Only the hush that drifted with the tide.

In that great stillness something in me heard,
The truth that loneliness outlives the word.

Yet even swallowed sound can still be song,
A note that proves the soul has stretched so long.

So in the silence born from whale and wave,
I found the beauty only vastness gave.

Currents Without Maps

No chart could name the waters where I drift,
The tide alone became my only gift.

The currents pulled through channels dark and wide,
Yet asked no fear, only the will to ride.

I could not see what waited far below,
Nor where the moonlit undertow might go.

Still something in the movement whispered peace,
A trust that not all journeys need release.

The sea has roads no compass learns to trace,
Invisible as memory, deep as grace.

Some truths arrive when direction falls away,
And all we have is water, night, and sway.

So I let go and followed what was true,
The nameless current carrying me through.

Freshwater

River Teeth

The river ran with silver, restless speed,
Yet caught on jagged memories like reed.

Dark branches jutted sharp from moving glass,
Like moments in the mind we cannot pass.

The current curled around each stubborn scar,
Still carrying its wound both near and far.

Some losses rise like driftwood through the stream,
Half buried in the flow, yet harshly seen.

The water learns to move through what it keeps,
Around the ache that snags, around what sleeps.

And still the river finds its onward way,
Though broken shapes refuse to drift away.

So life moves on, but not without the proof,
Of river teeth that catch beneath the truth.

Reflections in the Reed Glass

The pond lay still beneath the bending reed,
A mirror made for every thought and need.

My face appeared in trembling bands of light,
Half truth in day, half stranger in the night.

The water showed the lines I thought I knew,
Then bent them soft in shades of silver blue.

Each ripple changed the story of my name,
Yet somehow left the deeper self the same.

The reeds stood close like questions in the air,
Their whispering forms repeating what was there.

I leaned to see what silence might reveal,
A soul made clearer by what would not still.

So in that glass of water, dusk, and sky,
I met the self that never learned to lie.

Cattails and Ghosts

The cattails swayed beside the darkening shore,
Like hands that waved from childhood once before.

The marsh breathed out old voices with the mist,
Soft names and laughter time could not resist.

Each ripple carried footsteps through the reed,
A ghost of summer moving with the weed.

I thought I saw old shadows near the bank,
Where years had settled deep and memory sank.

The frogs called out like echoes from the past,
A song of things too fleeting long to last.

Yet nothing here felt cruel, only near,
The kind of haunting made from love and year.

So dusk and water held what I had lost,
And let it drift back gently through the frost.

The Current Knows Me

The river curled around my waiting feet,
A patient pull both tender and complete.

It moved as if it knew the shape I hide,
And drew me softly with its inward tide.

No map was needed for the way it ran,
It bent through stone with more than mortal plan.

Each turn it took became a lesson clear,
That change is only motion dressed as fear.

The water knew where every wound would rest,
And carried pain to places made for rest.

I let it take the names I could not save,
And watched them loosen into ripple and wave.

So now I trust what pulls beyond my sight,
The current knows the way through dark and light.

Stone Sleeps in the Stream

The river rushed with silver, foam, and flight,
Yet stones below held fast in silent light.

They rested where the strongest waters ran,
Unmoved beneath the force no hand could span.

The current sang above their patient sleep,
While stillness rooted downward, calm and deep.

No storm of rain, no thawing spring could break,
The quiet strength the river could not shake.

I saw in them the peace that movement hides,
A steadier truth beneath life's shifting tides.

For even where the loudest waters sweep,
The soul can find a place to rest and keep.

So now I trust the quiet at the core,
The stone that sleeps while all else moves once more.

Wetlands at Dusk

The marsh grew still beneath the violet sky,
As day exhaled and let the sunlight die.

The reeds stood dark like guardians of the shore,
While hidden wings stirred softly evermore.

Beneath the glass, small lives began to wake,
A secret pulse that twilight could not break.

The frogs sang low from pockets thick with green,
Their chorus blessing all that moved unseen.

The water held both shadow and rebirth,
A mirror for the changing face of earth.

What seemed at rest was rich with silent change,
A living hush both intimate and strange.

So dusk became the hour I trusted most,
Where endings bloom in every reed and ghost.

Mountain

Summit Breath

At last I stood where stone outclimbed the sky,
And drew the thinning air with grateful sigh.

The world below fell small in folds of green,
A distant life half remembered, half unseen.

Each breath arrived like mercy, sharp and clear,
A silence held between relief and fear.

The climb had carved its lesson into bone,
Yet here the mountain made the effort known.

No noise remained but wind and beating chest,
The pause between two heartbeats felt like rest.

From heights like this the burdens shifted shape,
Once felt endless now seemed small enough to escape.

So on the summit, breath became a prayer,
A quiet proof that peace still waits up there.

Where Sky Meets Bone

The ridge rose hard where cloud and granite blend,
A brutal path that seemed to never end.

Each handhold cut its lesson into skin,
A trial carved as much without as within.

The stone beneath my fingers held no grace,
Yet forced the soul to find its truest place.

Above, the sky stretched cold and fiercely near,
A height that sharpened every breath of fear.

The climb stripped comfort down to nerve and spine,
Until the body's ache became divine.

Where sky met bone, all falsehood fell away,
And only what was real had strength to stay.

So on that ledge between the earth and blue,
I found the part of me the mountain knew.

Stone as Old as Silence

The granite stood before the first dawn's light,
And kept its watch through every passing night.

The storms have come with thunder, snow, and rain,
Yet left the mountain rooted, vast, and plain.

Whole forests rose and vanished at its feet,
While stone remained unmoved through cold and heat.

The rivers carved their silver through its side,
Still age could not unmake its patient pride.

It knows the language only centuries keep,
A truth so old it settles into sleep.

All things around it hurry, bloom, and fade,
Yet mountain time moves slow in shadowed shade.

So standing there beside that ancient face,
I felt how stillness outlives speed and race.

Air This Thin is a Prayer

The higher slopes gave less with every breath,
Each inhale sharpened close to life and death.

The lungs reached out for what the sky would spare,
And found in hunger something close to prayer.

Each step became a plea the body made,
A vow of will that would not turn or fade.

The wind cut through the ribs with holy cold,
A sermon spoken sharper than the old.

No comfort lived this far above the trees,
Only the grace of breath earned on the freeze.

The struggle stripped the spirit down to need,
Until desire itself became the creed.

So in that thinning air I learned this truth,
The soul climbs highest when it leans on truth.

Alone in the Upward Wind

The path climbed steep through shale and broken stone,
A road of struggle meant for one alone.

No voice remained to tell me where to go,
Only the upward pull through ice and snow.

The wind pressed hard against my aching side,
Yet somehow gave me strength enough to stride.

Each step was mine, unseen by any eye,
A private war fought underneath the sky.

The mountain asks for all that fear would hide,
Then strips the soul until there's only pride.

No hand could share the burden of that height,
No witness saw the labor of the night.

So in the wind that climbed with me above,
I found my strength in solitude and love.

Ridge Line Psalm

The ridge ran thin along the edge of sky,
A place where earth and silence both run high.

The valleys fell in shadow far below,
While peaks still burned with evening's final glow.

No road remained beyond that narrow stone,
Only the hush of standing there alone.

The wind moved through the pines like whispered grace,
A psalm too old for words to fully trace.

So far from noise, the heart began to hear,
The sacred shape of everything made clear.

The world below grew small, yet somehow whole,
As distance opened deeper in the soul.

So on that line where sky and mountain blend,
I found a song that neither starts nor ends.

Volcanic Lands

Magma Beneath My Skin

A heat moved slow beneath the flesh and bone,
A buried fire that smoldered all alone.

No flame was seen, yet every nerve could feel,
The molten pulse beneath a cooling seal.

It gathered where old wounds refused to sleep,
In fault lines carved by hurts that settled deep.

The body held its mountains, calm and still,
While fire climbed upward with relentless will.

Each breath became a tremor under stone,
A warning that the quiet was not known.

What looked like peace was pressure learning form,
A hidden furnace building toward the storm.

So I walked on with embers in my veins,
A silent earth alive with buried flames.

The Ash Fell Like Confession

The mountain split and cast its hidden grief,
A blackened truth beyond all disbelief.

The ash came down in slow, accusing gray,
Like secrets we can no longer keep away.

Each drifting flake held something once concealed,
A wound, a name, a fear at last revealed.

The sky grew dark with everything unsaid,
A storm of truths long buried with the dead.

What fire began, the ash made plain to see,
The shape of all we were and failed to be.

It settled on the earth, on skin, on stone,
A quiet proof no soul erupts alone.

So in the fall of soot and shattered light,
I watched confession turn the dark to sight.

Born From Burned Ground

The ash lay thick where forests used to stand,
A blackened hush spread wide across the land.

No birds remained, no leaf, no shade, no song,
Only the silence after fire burned long.

Yet from the soot a fragile green would rise,
A tender shoot beneath the grieving skies.

The earth made room where all had turned to loss,
And stitched new life through every vein of moss.

What seemed like end became a fertile start,
A root reborn in ruin's broken heart.

The fire had stripped the false and left the true,
A place where something stronger now could grew.

So from the scars the living world returned,
Proof even hope can bloom from what was burned.

Where the Earth Broke Open

The ground gave way beneath my trusted feet,
A sudden fracture born of buried heat.

The fault ran wide and split the world in two,
A line between the old life and the new.

What once stood firm fell inward, stone by stone,
A breaking so complete it stood alone.

The fire below rose fierce enough to name,
The part of life no longer stayed the same.

There is a sound when certainty must bend,
A crack that marks the place where stories end.

Yet in that wound the earth revealed its core,
A truth more honest than the ground before.

So every life must learn this molten art,
Some worlds must split to show the hidden heart.

Fire Sleeps Below Us

The valley looked at peace beneath the sky,
A quiet place where nothing seemed to lie.

Yet under stone the old heat held its breath,
A patient force still warm beneath the depth.

The earth remembers every buried flame,
Each ancient wound still pulsing with its name.

No smoke arose, no tremor split the ground,
But still the hush carried a waiting sound.

Some dangers rest in silence, not in sleep,
A slow red pulse that settles dark and deep.

The calm above is only borrowed time,
A fragile peace held over hidden fire.

So every step upon the cooling plain,
Felt like a trust placed over living veins.

A Crater's Memory

The crater held the shape of what had been,
A hollow carved where fire once burned unseen.

Its walls stood black with echoes turned to stone,
A silent proof no wound survives alone.

The smoke was gone, the ash had found its rest,
And still the earth remembered all the pressed.

What violence tore had left a sacred ring,
A scar made wide enough for peace to sing.

No flame remained, yet warmth lived in the ground,
A gentler pulse beneath the quiet round.

The wound itself became a place to stay,
Where grief could settle, heal, and soften gray.

So standing at the rim of all that passed,
I learned that broken earth can still hold fast.

Afterword: What the Earth Left in Me

I leave these pages carrying root and flame,
No longer wholly separate from their name.

The forest kept its whispers in my chest,
The desert taught me how to survive the test.

The ice preserved the grief I could not bear,
The mountains gave my spirit thinner air.

The grasslands stretched my thoughts beyond the
known,
The rivers taught me how to keep still flowing.

The ocean showed that loss can still return,
The volcanic heart taught what must burn to learn.

Now every wind, each stone, each wave, each tree,
Still carries something wild inside of me.

So when the world grows loud and hard to see,
I'll listen for the earth still speaking free.

www.ingramcontent.com/pod-product-compliance
Lightning Source LLC
Chambersburg PA
CBHW031151250726
48655CB00002B/932